Lyrics for the album Carol + 44

by Svend Engh

© 2016 Svend-Erik Engh
Forlag: BoD, København, Danmark
Tryk: BoD, Norderstedt, Tyskland
ISBN 978-87-7145-840-4

Lyrics for the album Carol + 44

by Svend Engh

No. 1 is lyrics by Engh/Scbarff

No. 5 is lyrics by Emil Scharff Christensen

Front page of Carol, design Emil Scharff Christensen

Carol is a Vinyl LP with the one man band project called Wet Parsnip. Emil Scharff Christensen is songwriter, singer, producer and plays all instruments.

The Vinyl album Carol has a beautiful cover and you'll find the lyrics on the back, like in the old days.

You can order a signed copy for 200 kr. on www.svenderikengh.com - or you can play it on your electronic devices on Spotify. Search for Wet Parsnip and Carol.

This book contains all the lyrics to the songs in the Album + a number of other lyrics for songs written by Svend Engh.

The book is divided into three chapters:

Chapter one: Lyrics from the album Carol

Chapter two: Lyrics for songs you can find on Soundcloud, Yourlisten.com etc.

Chapter three: Lyrics, that still haven't got any tune. If you are interested in making a tune to one of the songs from chapter three, please contact Svend on see@historier.dk

Content

Chapter one

From the Vinyl Album – also available on Spotify – Carol with the one man band Wet Parsnip

1. **She Came Out Through the Bathroom Window**
2. **She Slammed the Door**
3. **Carol**
4. **Return in the Snow**
5. **My Sweetest Friend**
6. **Dead Man´s Waltz**
7. **Summer is Dead**
8. **Between Now and Then**
9. **How Could I Know?**

 *Illustration by Emil Scharff Christensen*

Chapter two

You can find these songs on Soundcloud or Yourlisten. Just use the link at the bottom of each page.

10. Harleen 1
11. Harleen 2
12. Orange fungus
13. I saw her leaving
14. New York, New York, soft version
15. Into the eyes
16. Sister
17. Johnny Rotten

Illustration by Alice Fernbank

Chapter three

These lyrics doesn't have a tune yet. If you are a musician and will create a tune to one song, write me a mail: see@historier.dk

31. Fox is out tonight
32. Invitation of Lucifer's eye
33. Angels
34. Many great patriots #34
35. In a blink of an eye
36. Archie hits back
37. Ben's boat
38. The tree
39. In front of a café
40. A rainy day somewhere
41. Teacher said
42. It is clear
43. BZ
44. Open your eyes, stranger!
45. In between reality
46. In France there were no regrets
47. Edinburgh's hgruhnide
48. New York, New York, funky version
49. I aint gonna work for the US government no more
50. Red haired giant
51. Blind trust
52. Buzzard
53. Pure gold

Chapter 1

**From the Vinyl Album – also available on Spotify –
Carol with the one man band Wet Parsnip**

1. She Came Out Through the Bathroom Window

Lyrics by Engh and Scharff[1]

She came out through the bathroom window
The war was all around
She never heard a whisper, she never heard a sound
The war was all around

It was like a waterfall
And the rainbow was so clear

Although the canons fired, she felt no fear
'Cause she had heard the music in her ear
The thing you could compare to the life above

Water pouring tenderly was something she could hear
And the pretty birds singing in her ear

She left the land and went away
She still hasn't been seen to this day
She left from here, but she must be somewhere
Maybe she's just floating in the air

---

[1] Emil and Svend were both working on Ebberoed and one day at the dinner Emil asked Svend, if he could write lyrics for a song. The Beatles was and is a major inspiration for both and this day the song 'She came out through the bathroom window' was alive. Svend imagined the girl from the song of Lennon/Mcartney leave the house after 60 years and therefore he wrote the 1. line of the song: 'She came out through the bathroom window'

2. She Slammed the Door

She slammed the door and left him there
Pale face in the light from the moon
She looked around and saw her world
And saw it had changed into a cartoon
The suburban street in front of her
Filled with cars made to forget
The colors of the fifties
Bright shining yellow and red

Chorus
In the valley lies the forest
Silverlight, flesh and bones
It was time for her to choose
Between the rocks and stones

She felt the cold of the night
As she reached the end of the street
She turned around and saw him there
Looking helpless from head to feet
As she reached the end of the line
She felt the bones under her shoes
The fear was something she could face
She had to find a way to handle the blues

Chorus

The house collapsed and the walls fell down
Dust was spread everywhere
On the shelf, a photo was there
Showing a bride with pearls in her hair
She slammed the door and left him there
Pale face in the light from the moon
She looked around and saw her world
And saw it had changed into a cartoon

Chorus

3. **Carol**

You said you were finished with men
I said "yeah, sure" and kissed you again
You asked me if I didn't hear what you just said
I said "yeah, sure" and had you on my bed

Chorus
Carol, you are the proudest girl I've ever seen
Carol, everything about you is a loving Queen
Carol, your mouth tastes of red strawberry
Carol, indeed you are dear and merry

After one year you were still on my bed
I think it's true, the thing that you said
That you were done with foolish men
I just hope that I'm not one of them

Chorus
Carol, when you shower I wait outside
Carol, whenever you smile I see the light
Carol, your skin is soft and sweet
Carol, everything about you is neat

Chorus
Carol, a shining diamond is what you are
Carol, you are a glooming Star
Carol, your body is out of sight
Carol, I think about you day and night

4. **Return in the snow**

In the middle of a good old fight
I saw the light
It was the torch in your heart
I saw you fell apart

Then you gave me a golden ring
Said it was the thing
To prove your honor and name
I saw the burning flame

I wish I shouldn't explain
In the pouring rain
Why we had to say goodbye
Tears in your eye

I told you, I was the sea
Plain as can be
My tatoos were exquisite and wild
Yours like a little child

So I boarded a thousands ships
And kissed your lips
Left for the harbours of Puorto Rico
My name was Chigo

You called me the other day
Said you had to say
That our son will definitely grow
Please return in the snow

5. **[2]My Sweetest Friend**

I've been traveling a million miles
Just to see you face again
And I've been going around the earth for some time
To see if I am still the man I was back then

I've been running around for ages
Looking for a smile so hard to get
And I've been forced to follow rivers to the end
To see if I can hear your voice again, my sweetest friend

---

[2] Lyrics by Emil Scharff Christensen

6. **Dead Man's Waltz**

The town I live in
Progress on halts
People being busy
Dancing the dead man's waltz

Walking the main road
Filled with old Renaults
All you can hear is radios
Playing the dead man's waltz

I wish I could leave
After a few assaults
Chase all the ghosts
Silence the dead man's waltz

But now is time for feast
No more playing false
Every soul in town
Celebrating the dead man's waltz

I dance and I dance
With a woman so cold
I am learning the steps
Of the good old rock n' roll

It is furious and wild
I do my somersaults
I whirl on my toes
Living the dead man's waltz

Trying to escape
Jumping in vaults
Arms holding firm
Forcing the dead man's waltz

I wake up alone
Empty town exalts
No people, only skulls
Dancing the dead man's waltz

7. **Summer is dead**

Summer is dead
September instead
Rain pouring down
Destroying summers crown

No children on the beach
You can feel winter reach
Out for your warmth and glow
Soon covered in the snow

Did you win the battles to win
Salty water on brown skin
In the heat of the night
Making love in the moon light

Did you do all that
Did you have the chat
The deep talk in the warm sunset
You better, 'cause summer is dead

8. Between now and then

Between now and then
Between where and when
Between father and boy
Between anger and joy
You will find me disarmed

Between narrow and wide
Between modesty and pride
Between infinity and the end
Between love and a friend
You will find me all mixed up

Chorus
When you ask me if I am ready to see
What happens when love is given to me
Then I am a coward amongst men
So I stand here in the end, right between now and then

Between high and low
Between arrow and bow
Between earth and the sky
Between where and why
You will find me bewildered

Between a tune and a song
Between old and young
Between fear and hope
Between clean and dope
You will find me longing

Chorus

9. How could I know?

A boy reaches out to touch a hot burning stow
Mother shouts: "Don't do it! It's a no go"
Boy do it, you know the old refrain
A man has to feel. He has to feel his own pain

Mother while shaking her head: "Didn´t I tell you so?"
Boy with cries out: "But how could I know?"

A teenage girl comes home late at night
She's been crying, you can see it in the light
Father steps in. He is shaking his head
"Don´t", she says, "comfort me instead"

Her father is trying his best: "Didn't I tell you so?"
The girl cries out: "But how could I know?"

Chorus
"How could I, how could I, how could I, how could I know?"

A woman comes to the hospital every day
To visit her husband who is far away
He is cracked by a war a thousand miles out there
Every day she finds him on the same ugly chair

The woman while screaming for help: "Didn't I tell you so?"
He looks back with nothing in his eyes: "How could I know?"

Chorus

Solo

I have a strange dream. The end of the world in my face
The animals gathers and say goodbye to the human race
They just stands there with a sadness in their eyes
As the rocket ship leaves with the human lies

The animals while looking at us: "Didn't we tell you so?"
Sitting in the space ship we all agree: "How could we
know?"

Chorus
How could we, how could we, how could we, how could we
know?"

Illustration by Emil Scharff Christensen

Chapter 2

You can find these songs on Soundcloud or Yourlisten. Just use the link at the bottom of each page.

10. [3]Harleen (no. 1)

You stumbled into my life one sunny afternoon
You said you would like to learn how to howl at the moon
Somebody had told you I was good at that howling stuff
You looked awful disappointed when I said "Wasn't that tough"
I tried to please you and said lets tell a story or two
After you had finished your story I was hopelessly in love with you

Chorus
Harleen, you never noticed
I fell to the ground
Harleen, at that moment
I felt like a stupid clown

Later that evening, when jokes were told
You laughed and your eyes sparkled like gold
I couldn't help dreaming about that look in your eyes
I started flying and soon found myself high up in the skies

Chorus
Harleen, you never saw me
hanging there in the clouds
Harleen, you were too busy
talking to some scouts

---

[3] There are two versions of this song. This version is recorded by Svend-Erik Engh:
https://soundcloud.com/svend-erikengh/harleen

As the week went on we went swimming in the sea
The red sun went down and painted the sky dramatically
The salty water held our bodies floating in a spin
I felt like drowning when I touched your soft skin

Chorus
Harleen, I think I dreamed
about that touch
Harleen, anywy
I enjoyed it so much

Every good thing comes to an end now we are back in our
reality
I am sitting here writing this song and working on my
identity
Its to hard to realize that the whole love affair was just a
dream
Something that went on inside my imaginary screen

Chorus
Harleen i will learn how to howl some crazy day
Harleen I know its going to be okay in any way

Now I'm howling and dancing as the days goes on
So I will be prepared next time you come along

Chorus

11. [4]**Harleen (no.2)**

Harleen, you came into my life one sunny afternoon
You said you would like to learn how to howl at the moon
I said I didn't know anything about howling stuff
You said it was just a question of being cool enough
I tried to please you and said let's tell a story or two
After we were done I was hopelessly in love with you

Chorus
Harleen, you never noticed
I fell to the ground
Harleen, at that moment
I felt like a stupid clown

Later that evening, when jokes were told
You laughed and your eyes sparkled like gold
I couldn't help dreaming about that look in your eyes
I started flying and found myself high up in the skie

Chorus
Harleen, you never saw me
hanging there in the clouds
Harleen, you were too busy
talking to some scouts

As the week went on and we went swimming in the sea
The red sun went down and painted our sky dramatically
The salty water held our bodies floating in a spin
I felt like drowning when I touched your soft skin

---

[4] This version is by Emil Scharff Christensen:
https://is.gd/QgU8bG

Chorus
Harleen, I think I dreamed
about that touch
Harleen, anywy
I enjoyed it so much

Solo
Chorus
Harleen i will learn how to howl some crazy day
Harleen I know its going to be okay in any way

Now we are back in our reality
I am sitting here working on my identity
Its to hard to realize that the whole love affair was just a
dream
Something that went on inside my imaginary screen

Chorus

Harleen i will learn howl at the moon with you
at the moon with you
at the moon with you

Harleen i wanna howl at the moon with you
at the moon with you
at the moon with you

12. [5]Orange fungus

Climate change is here for good
It is well understood
No rain in whole of July
And you could hear the trees cry
Out for some lifegiving water
Calling out for Angeronas[6] daughter

This weekend the drought ended
for the trees and the people mended
The rain poured down in bars
With thunder and dust from Mars
Monday I made my run as I always do
Then I saw something I will share with you

A fungus so orange and self confident
Like a gigantic solar rose bent
Over what was left of a tree
Like it had been there since eternity

Yet I know I was told
That fungus was only three days old
Shining, shining like the purest gold

---

[5] Play it:
http://www.dr.dk/musik/karrierekanonen/#!/band/wetpars
nip/track/21508

[6] Roman goddess for water

That fungus made me think
If a fungus can wait for a drink
One whole month for a drop
In nature there is no stop
When all the human fuzz is gone
Nature will rise again, a new dawn

13. [7]I saw her leaving

She fled from her house through the chimney
Determinated to follow her own heartbeat
She found a ladder going up to the sun
So she started climbing, allways on the run

As the ladder reached Venus, the evil twin
She couldn't breathe, the air burned within
She reached Mercury turning so slow
At this point her spirit was so low

Chorus

The sun was shining oh so bright
In her heart it was the darkest night
She took it out to see the light
And everybody screamed: That girl has gone crazy

She turned around to get as far
Away as possible from the burning star
Her mother shouted: 'Behave and dress well'
She cried back: 'Mother, go to hell'

She passed through the man in the moon
and saw it was nothing but a big, smiling baloon
The red dust of Mars filled her with fear
Her screaming voice nobody could hear

Chorus

---

[7] Play it here: https://is.gd/QgU8bG

She whirled through the astroides of this heaven
She asked for a prince but a fox was given
The wind of Jupiter in a perfect form
In her mind she could feel the storm

As she cut herself on the sharp ring of Saturn
She saw it through, the shaped pattern
She knew it was time to say goodbye
And I just stood there didn't know why

Chorus

I saw her leaving
I saw her leaving
I saw her leaving
I saw her leaving

14. [8]New York, New York, soft version

A visit to a sleepless city
A town not worth the pity
People in New York rest
When the time is best

New York October town
Circus spinning round
Woman on bike so insequre
Help me find a cure

Chorus
I spend my day walking
In underground trains talking
A endless talk
New York, New York

Times Square
Yes, I was there
Times left you unreal
That's what we all feel
Memorial full of tear
Take a snap or a year
Taxi driver all the way from Kentucky
To buy things to feel lucky

Chorus

---

[8] Play it: https://soundcloud.com/thypsychisacoustic/new-york-demo

15. [9]In the eyes of

In the eyes of a blind man
A future in peace
He was the only one I met
Believed war could cease

In the eyes of a believer
I saw no room for any doubt
And it made me worry
It made me wanna shout

Chorus
In the eyes

In the eyes of a stock broker
I noticed nothing to tell
In the eyes of a child
He was clever as hell

In the eyes of a tiger
I saw a mighty king
And the King was now
A worthless thing

Chorus

---

[9] Play it: https://soundcloud.com/thypsychisacoustic/in-the-eyes-demo-1

In the eyes of a stranger
I saw friendship grow
In the eyes of a politiceman
Promises from long ago

In the eyes of a woman
Longing for better days
Her mind so full of trouble
She didn't know her ways

Chorus

16. [10]Sister

My mothers tears
In all those years
Was shown to none
She turned to run
My father quiet
Inside a riot
Didn't say a word
The clock he heard

Chorus
When I was five I was told
That my sister was sick
She was only nine years old
The clock went tick tack tick

The illness to call
Red spot on a wall
Animal sinister
Inside my sister
When she died
We all cried
I never heard
A comforting word

Chorus x 2

---

[10] Play it:
http://www.dr.dk/musik/karrierekanonen/#!/band/wetpars
nip/track/21506

17. [11]Johnny Rotten

Johnny was rotten
He had totally forgotten
How to threat a lady like you should
His wife Lucy
Once sommersweet and juicy
Working as hard as she could
Every day Johhny sat in his bar
Telling stories how he used to be a star
How he was a rocksinger - the best of his kind
Untill Lucy came around and blew his mind

Chorus
Oh Johnny why wont you come home
Oh Johnny I lay here on my own
Oh Johnny how can I ever find rest?
Oh Johnny you are still the best

Solo

Chorus
Oh Johnny why wont you come home
Oh Johnny I lay here on my own
Oh Johnny how can I ever find rest?
Oh Johnny you are still the best

---

[11] Play it: https://is.gd/rylhAT

One night three men walked in
A small guy with two guards on his chin
The bar grew quiet and the little man spoke
"Johnny, take of that hat
lets have a chat
When we are finished with our little talk
I want you to get up and walk
Out that door and never come back for more fun.
I buy you a drink – your last one"

Chorus

The little man said
"What is going on your head?
Lucy chose you from a houndred of men
And I have asked myself again and again
What she saw in you and that singing voice
But I allways respected her choice
Untill I met her the other day
She looked tired as hell and therefore I say
Now you go home and threat your lady
The way a man should threat his lady."

Chorus

Johnny got up and the men in the bar
Looked at him like they did when he was a star
But now Johnny was feeling really rotten
And he had totally forgotten
How to make an exit with grace
So he just stumpled and smashed his face

As he bumped into the door
And fell head down on the floor
He heard the barman say: go, go, go
How he got home he didn't know

Chorus

Lucy was allways awake
When Johnny came in drunk´n shake
Every night he just tumbled in
Stinking of gin
But this night he said
While he sat on the side of the bed
"You can go to sleep now, Lucy
I am all right
Nothing had happened to me this night"
So Lucy turned around
To that very unfamiliar sound
Johnnys face looked like shit
And Johnny didn´t know what to do
Happily his left arm knew

Chorus
Oh Johnny I am so glad you are home
Oh Johnny I been laying here on my own
Oh Johnny now I can find rest
Oh Johnny you are still the best

Illustration by Alice Fernbank

Chapter 3

These lyrics doesn't have a tune yet. If you are a musician and will create a tune to one (or more) of the songs, write me a mail: see@historier.dk

18. The front seat

Ever since I was a little boy
I was on the backseat
My sister sat in the front
I could feel the heat

The talk went on and on
Just like I feared
Ma and sister ignored
That I was feeling weird

Later, when I became older
I met a beautiful girl
She said you can sit in the back
Let's give it a whirl

But for me it was the whole thing
I couldn't sit and curl
I told her she was my light
Next day I dumped that pearl

Solo
Now I am lonely as can be
But I am in the frontseat
I enjoy every step of the ride
I feel my heart beat

I will drive all alone
Untill I will meet you
We will share the frontseat
And together enjoy the view

19. **Clive´s hat**

Clive out of law school nothing but A´s
Future containing only sunny days
His life seemed like a living dream
One day he woke up with a scream

He was terrified with remorse and shame
A discrase for his family name
It was a gag only made for fun
But it made Clive in pain turned to run

It started one evening as the greatest ball
No sign of danger on the Clivean wall
Clive and his friends from the school
Crossed a park, met an old ragged fool

Clive was drunk and generously tough
He Couldn´t be cruel and mean enough
So Clive ran and pissed on the old mans hat
Old fool did not respond to that

It was a turning point for wonderboy Clive
And within a month helplessly he dived
Into a deep hole of fear and agony
The old fool´s eyes made Clive to see

If you are on your way to the top
Act decent to people on your way up
One day he had suffered enough
His friends laughed: 'World´s rough!'

Clive was desperate so he went
And found the old fools tent
Asked if the fool knew of Clive´s pain
Growing so fast inside his brain

Old man didn´t have anything to say
Clive said he was sorry for that day
The old fool just handed over his hat
Now it was Clives turn to wear that

20. Love is all you need

Chorus
I am going to San Fransisco
It'll be fifty years too late
I am going to my dream city
Below the Golden Gate

I was born in the wrong time
I am a stranger to this world
I don't belong here, I'm out of tune
My cloth too colored, my hair too curled

Chorus

Music today is pure cash
In those days it was the real thing
They loved what they did, so do I
Music today is no but a lie

Chorus

The way I dream things should be done
Where all people should make friends
Love should be spread all over the world
Love power will win in all ends

Chorus

21. **Derived ugly disguise**

Only look into this gap
Postponed within
Alone without reason together
Our bodies in a twitch
As blind corpus in affect
Sweating skin that curls
Screaming our common code
A sudden transformation

Bing

Out violate one
And only one
Spitting dwarf
The dwarf dribbles and says nicely Pardon
Every time someone steps on it

22. **When Messiah comes**

It happened on a Tuesday night
Before eight pm
A man walked on the water
Made the world a claim

He was the brand new Messiah
Back to save our day
He would change war into peace
He would show the way

Chorus
When Messiah comes
When Messiah comes
When Messiah comes

TV reporters all wondered
If he had holes in his feet
Before Messiah could answer
They all went for a threat

A couple of days passed
And the world lost its grib
It was only on Twitter
Messiah still was hip

Chorus

To make Beaujolais out of water
From the polluted Rhine
Was fun years ago - it
Didn't make him shine

So people said to Messiah
"Hey, man, make a feast"
I swear to God he tried
To make peace in the Middle East

Chorus

Messiah stumbled
And fell to the ground
Nobody heard his crying
Nobody heard a sound

So now he is forgotten
World found a new toy
A saver that can do tricks
Messiah works as a boy

Chorus

23. **I was waiting**

I was waiting for the yellow buss
I was waiting for my love to shine
Home town to be impressed
By the love of mine

I was waiting

While I was waiting people passed by
Knowing nothing of the importance
Of the moment
Ignorant fools

Time stopped
Yellow bus over the hill
On the main street
Bartender asked me to pay the bill

I was waiting

As the buss emptied
I couldn't breath
A stream of people
A river beneath

As the yellow bus drove on
And no love in sight
I phoned my love to hear
The words that created night

She wasn't going to show up
Found another from another hood
So all my friends came around
None of them understood

Why I was waiting

Now I am sitting here
Begging for hope and money
Busses passes by on schedule
Still waiting for my honey

I am waiting

24. **Her dream**

When she woke up
From her horror night mare
She saw him lying there
In her single bed so rare

She couldn't remember
His face, his body, his feet
And told him to leave
Just split, she said in a tweet

He said they had made love
And had held each other tight
Instead of leaving he would
Listen to her dream from night

She told him he was crazy
And that he just had to leave
He stretched his long body
Told her to trust and to give

And so she told him
About her dream so scary
About the monsters
So ugly, wild and hairy

For nearly one hour
She told him, shaked
Scared the life out
Of her to be that naked

He was a clever guy
So for one day he could stay
That way he could listen
To a new dream every day

25. **Steve's dream**

Chorus
Every night Steve had the same dream
Every morning he woke up with a scream
Breath like a typhoon, huh huh huh
Calling out for someone, you you you

In the dream ten years old
Looking for the hidden gold
In the garden of his mother
All alone, there were no other
To break the perfect harmony
Of the roses, white beauty
Mother out with lemonade
To drink it in the shade

Chorus

Suddenly opened a hole
Yellow lemonade so cold
Dancing on mothers hips
A question on mothers lips
Her face showing surprise
As a roar beneath arise
Mother disappeared into dark
Garden turned into a park

Chorus

No trace of hole in the ground
Steve looked all around
No help from people passing by
They were gazing into the sky
Where an eagle chased a hawk
Steve looked up, couldn't talk
The eagle catched the hawks tale
And changed into a giant whale

Chorus

Steve felt hands grapping his pants
He saw his mothers hands
Pulling him down into the hole
Dragged a hole in his soul
The whale landed on his shoulder
His mother looking so much older
The weight killed him right away
As night turned into day

Chorus

26. Grandma

Grandma is dying
Mother is crying
Quiet is the little girl

Mother in despair
Pulls out her hair
"It's the end of the world"

Grandma makes a sigh
"Don't you cry
It's just me dying

It's going to be
OK - look up and see
And stop your weeping crying"

The stories are cool
She went to school
Searching for love and peace

Universal truth
In their youth
Made the worlds release

Dreams of gem
Times gave them
A powerful new song

Little girl laughs
Grandma coughs
The whole day long

Solo

Grandma died
Mother cried
Little girl shed a tear

Friends salute
Grandma's tribute
Mothers sigh in your ear

Mother screamed "no
It was to early to go
It doesn't make any sense"

Fair and bold
Little girl told
Grandmas stories emmence

Spoken:
All the people attending Grandma's funeral laughed at the
little girl's stories from Grandma's past
Mother felt it was very wrong to laugh at a funeral

27. It is a transition

I am alive and well
It is simple as hell
You might think it will last
But no, things like that changes fast
And it's just a transition

My mother feared my birth
The result was not the pain worth
Doctor came in
stinking of gin
Chewing gum
Said to my mum
it is a transition

After fifty minutes in pain
I came out, I think in vain
They looked at me:
What's he gonna be?
Can he walk?
Can he talk?
it is a transition

I started wondering like them
Would I become trash or a gem?
Would I shave?
Be bold and brave?
Have a style?
Worth while?
it is a transition

In spring the forest is green and soft
it is a transition

A war began another had an end
I had my TV on it was my friend
Bombs in hair
Bombs everywhere
Soldiers Children
Womens men
it is a transition

I left my family and moved into town
I learned to swim I didn't drown
Never satisfied
So I cried
I wanted more
Of lifes core
It is a transition

The cold war made us freeze
A wall came down, what a release
A minute or more
No cold war
Peace on what
We called "our world"
it is a transition

Loose yourself, you reappear
Suddenly you find have nothing to fear
it is a transition
The fear will come back to you
it is a transition

I fell in love so deep and true
I was really in love with you
I don't lie
You made me cry
Then times pass
And so did our love
it is a transition

In Beijing you cannot breathe the air
It changed when Obama was there
When he was in town
No cars was found
No factories
They could all breathe
it is a transition

Somewhere a child is born
The baby is fresh and kind
it is a transition

In France things never will be the same
It is such a pity, such a shame
12 people died that day
Because they had something to say
That made hate come alive
Bang, a crying wife
it is a transition

I see people commit in large scope
To a brighter future, they're full of hope
He knows
She knows
They know
We know
it is a transition

I turn around and a dark future arouses
They talk about it in their cartoon houses
Is even worse
They spit and curse
Hell is here
Full of hate and fear
It is a state of fact and no transition

The evening sun never ever more beautiful
it is a transition

I promised you an ending of this song
I promise you now it won't take long
I will soon be on my way
And to the very day
When we meet again
I will think of you as a friend
it is a transition

So now I am old, alone and wise
(or at least that is what I think I am)
You saw right through my diguise
(and you said it in a very low voice)
Hey, old man, you're just a fool
In lifes school
You have a little boy inside
That is hoping to see the light
it is a transition

28. **The end**

The world looses control
Blame it on the rock'n roll
On the edge we all dance
Like it is our last chance
We are looking for a glimpse of hope
Hanging out from the end of a rope
Wishing we were born and still alive
Counting down: ten, eight, seven, five

"And if my thoughtdreams could be seen
They'd probably put my head into a guillotine
But it's alright, Ma, it's life, and life only"
Somebody said that

Sometimes I dream
I was born in another world
With songs that meant something
Let the words into your heart
A new world will unfold
I said that

Chorus
No hope for the future
Time just stays the same
End of the world
I am looking for someone to blame

Every day a new disaster
We are going down faster and faster
I'm sitting on my chair
In and output everywhere
Sun descend without a sound
Police trying to be on the ground
We are in this together
A man talking about the weather
Can't blame him, he is a good guy
Please don't ask me how I know
He is actually talking about something
That matters to you and me
And whatever you say,
it is not that hard to see
"That you dont need a weatherman to
know which way the wind blows"
Somebody said that

Well, the wind blows
And the snow snows
It is plain to see
Nothing of that
Made any sense to me
I said that

Chorus
No hope for the future
Time just stays the same
End of the world
I am looking for someone to blame

As the dance ends
And we become friends
We sing out loud
Find a way to become proud

"Some speak of the future
My love she speaks softly"
Somebody said that

We can find a way
To make tomorrow a better day
I said that

Chorus
Hope for the future
Time never stays the same
Beginning of a new world
End of the no solutions game

29. **A nightmare**

I dreamt a dream that made me feel
Like I was in a spooky acid-trip
Like Lucy in the Sky so real
Hippie di hip hip hip hip

As I said I had a dream
I woke up with a scream
I went downstairs to see
If the dream was reality
Much to my delight it wasn´t at all
This is my nightmare as I recall

Well, in the dream my alarm clock rang
And my daily routine began
I took a shower
Brushed my teeth
Had some cofee
Walked the dogs
Woke the kids
Kissed my wife
Hurried down the suburban life

Hippie di hip hip hip
Hippie di hip hip hip
In the train

Outside rain
Read a paper (free)
Answered mails on my cell phone
Left the train
Wet from rain
Went inside
A tall office building
Had some more cofee
Talked a while
Gave a smile
Opened my labtop
Sat there for two hours or more
Had some lunch
Answered my phone
A meeting was held
Then another
And to finish my day
I opened my laptob again
And sat there for a full hour
Then I rushed to the train
More rain
Noticed someone reading a paper book, strange

Hippie di hip hip hip
Hippie di hip hip hip
In the train

Saxophone solo

Got inside my house
Had dinner
Asked questions to the kids
Watched TV
Opened my labtop for the last time that day
Answered more mails on my phone
Went to bed
Kissed my wife
And just before I fell asleep in my dream
I woke up with a scream
I just hope I will not dream
Anything as scary as this again

Hippie di hip hip hip
Hippie di hip hip hip
Till the end

30. I am not a whore

Chorus
I am not a whore
I am not a whore
I am not a whore
How many times do I have to repeat it?
Believe me!
I am not a whore

Poul was nineteen
Laura was yesterdays queen
On a date site
She invited him to Rome
Better than staying home
He realized she had a plan
She was a woman, he was a man
At the hotel, the Dormio Angeta
They should sleep together
"In the cosy room", she said
"There were only one bed"
Well, sleep they didn´t do much
She was all over him, she had that crush
In the elevator
In a Taxi, In the pool
She was hot. He was cool
When he'd got home
A friend asked: "Have u been to Rome?
How could u afford that?
And wow, what an expensive hat
Shirt and jeans, brand new
Tell me, man, who did u screw?"

Chorus

Josefine was sixteen
Pure and clean
Simon, twentynine was he
Had a car, a limo to be
She sat in his car
Like a moviestar
He had stacked very neat
A lot of stuff in the back seat
A Gucci, a phone so handy
She just had to be a little dandy
So she took him in the mouth
It wasn't the hole down south
It was OK, she said to Simon
She still had that virgin hymen
When her friends came to visit
All the stuff exquisite
Showed to be fake
laughed at her mistake
She blossomed with anger
When they said: "You are a wanker!"

Chorus

31. Fox is out tonight

The fox was out that night
I saw the red light
In the sunset
I did my little walk
I went down to the chicken yard
to have a little talk
With all my hens and all my chickens
And of course the cockroach
That night I could feel a tension
Something was wrong
Something terrible was going to happen

Chorus
The fox was out that night
I saw the red light

I checked the chicken yard
The fences, the bolt on the door
And after that there were no more
Things I could do so
I went inside the house
Had coffee and watched TV
Then I heard the noise
Went out to check
The hens were all sitting
Quiet as a graveyard
No sight of the red devil
But I was sure

Chorus

I fell asleep on the sofa with the TV on
I dreamt a terrible dream
With dead hens alle over,
Foxes eating them all
Blood everywhere
And the screaming hens woke me up

Chorus
It was morning
The sun was rising
I ran down to the chickenyard
I found all my hens in a state of shock
They were all sitting there
With a paralyzed look
No eggs no nothing
Just a bunch of paralyzed hens

Chorus
The fox had been out that night
There was a red light

For twelve days the hens were sitting there
On the twelfth day they all died
I buried them in the field
Sold my farm
And moved into the city

Chorus

32. Invitations of Lucifers eye

The invitations of Lucifers eye
Was sent to all my excited friends
Telling where and how and when
A celebration to life ends

As I unfolded the bow of Shiva
Just to impress my loved one
She looked at me with pearly eyes
Handed me a black gun
I said, I never had used such a toy
She laughed with her eyes full of joy
"You should not play with the thing
Just use it in the end"

Then Lucifer stepped up with his
Golden eye fixed on her belly
He raised his voice in a moment
Promising eternal life to every soul present
All should stay the same
Nothing should change

All my friends and their lovers
And a few wise men left over
Bursted out in joyful cries
And the phony appetizer said:
"Are you a man or a cow?"

So I pointed the gun into nowhere
And fired just for fun
And she sat there grinning
With three eyes in her face
As she fell over the collapsed floor
I ran to what was left of the door

The man in the hall cried out:
"You can never leave"
I felt betrayed and so did we all
That in a second believed
That something in this universe
Would stay the same!
And we all heard was Lucifer
As he laughed his head of
Some said they only heard
The sound of the rolling head

33. Angels

Once I had pilgrims
Running on my back
They jumped and they rolled
On my bad conscience
I had my hands out
Begging into the night
All I could hear was a whisper
"No mercy, no regrets"

Chorus
I saw all the pilgrims
Floating like angels
In the cold polluted water
Untill everything went quiet

I saw their tongues becoming black
When they turned their pages
They told me to be
Like all the rest
And I really
Tried my best
But their rules
Never came under my skin

Chorus

I drowned them
One windy day in September
So I returned to my home
Looked into the mirror
Much to my surprise
There were devils, monkeys
And reckless whores
Sitting on my left shoulder

Chorus

God, I miss my pilgrims

34. **Many Grey Patriots' 16**
   Written the 14th of January 2015

   In a dream
   I was sitting
   In a waiting room
   Somewhere on a planet
   Rushing through space

   A man from a different world
   Cleaned the floor
   For used cigarettes
   He didn't say a word
   But I swear I heard music in my ears
   Coming from a place deep below
   The sound of a saxophone
   A drum, a fiddle
   Somebody played on a harp

   Then the man with the broom
   Turned into a magician
   His broom whirled in the air
   And in the end it pointed at me

The man from the other side
Looked through my disguise
And I whispered "Sorry"
Felt naked as a child
Again "Sorry", this time a little louder
I screamed my apologies into the space
"I am so sorry", I shouted it and meant every word
The man turned, smiled and swept forward

With his broomstick taking away
The last used cigarettes
I turned to my coffee, drank it with delight
On that waiting room, that night, that moment
Speeding through the universe

35. **In a blink of an eye**

She made him go insane
By crawling into his brain
In a blink of an eye
She had that blue dress on
Made only for fun
In a blink of an eye
She moved her body so firm
Like a cat, like a worm
In a blink of an eye
Her eyes sparkled with joy
He was her little toy
In a blink of an eye

To the audience:
We are all going to do "The blink of an eye-dance"
Find a beautiful person next to you - look at that person -
Close your eyes
And then on the drums mark
Make one blink of an eye
Look how that beautiful person is mowing, dancing
That´s it. Have your eyes closed for a few seconds more.
Focus on what you saw on that blink of an eye.
Now - Open your eyes and the song will continue:

He was wearing shirt and a tie
She never asked why
In a blink of an eye
She took him by surprise
He felt his temperature rise
In a blink of an eye
Her body was a piece of art

He felt the beat of her heart
In a blink of an eye
He stood there paralized
He was totally mesmerized
In a blink of an eye
She was oh so close
Smelled like a rose
In a blink of an eye
Softly she took his hand
He did not understand
In a blink of an eye
She took it just to place
It on her bosoms grace
In a blink of an eye
He nearly died that day
She had him her way
In a blink of an eye
They made love that night
To the first morning light
In a blink of an eye

To the audience:
We are all going to do "The blink of an eye-dance"
Find a beautiful person next to you - look at that person -
Close your eyes
And then on the drums mark
Make one blink of an eye
Look how that beautiful person is mowing, dancing
That's it. Have your eyes closed for a few seconds more.
Focus on what you saw on that blink of an eye.
Now - Open your eyes and the song will continue:

To this very day
She dance her life away
In a blink of an eye
He is going to work
As a desk clerk
In a blink of an eye
But when he comes home
She is there on her own
In a blink of an eye
And they will dance
He will give it a chance
In a blink of an eye
He will moves his hips
And she will kiss his lips
In a blink of an eye
She will dance and forget
He will dance and regret
In a blink of an eye
And they will make more love
And the next door neighbours
Will complain like they always do
And they fall asleep
With a happy smile
And that is how good as it can be
To fall asleep and be so hap hap happy
So they live their lifes
And see times go by
Like a blink of an eye

To the audience:
We are all going to do "The blink of an eye-dance"
Find a beautiful person next to you - look at that person -

Close your eyes
And then on the drums mark
Make one blink of an eye
Look how that beautiful person is mowing, dancing
That´s it. Have your eyes closed for a few seconds more.
Focus on what you saw on that blink of an eye.
Now - Open your eyes and the song will end:

36. **Archie hits back**

Chorus
Archie got one year for domestic violence
All the way Archie kept his silence
He couldn´t tell them
He´d only defended his life
If he did they have to accuse his wife

Rosie and Archie was married in Maine
Honeymoon on Virgin Islands, days of rain
Rosie was strong and healthy
Knew how she liked things to be
Archie was a soft member of the human race
On the fifth day she slapped him
Right in the face
Filled with remorse
She kissed him in vain
And promised it would never happen again

Chorus

One day after two years of beating
Archie was so tired of self defeating
On his way from work he heard
A song in the radio
About a woman called Luca
And how it was
So late at night
When Rosie wanted to fight
He just said no,
You have to let go
And when Rosie slapped his face
He just punched back into space

Chorus

Photos: Sara Simone Engh

37. Bens Boat

Ben sat on his boat so fine
A twenty Benetau's smooth line
Drinking his afternoon pine
Enjoying the smell from the brine

Whirling dreams on waves of trust
Ben saw a woman's face on the gust
Into his ship she would enter just
To get rid of all Ben's rust

Chorus
That day it all happened on Ben´s boat
It was a fairy tale, a true anecdote

A sea gull did a shit on his deck
It was a disgusting, brown fleck
Changing the boat into a wreck
Then he heard it: 'What the heck'

A little boy raced down the pier
Chased by bigger boys, made Ben fear
That he was forced to interfere
So he stood there, rubbing his ear

Chorus

The little boy turned around
Made a very naughty sound
Then jumped into the water pound
Leaving the boys on the ground

For thirty seconds Ben stared
Into the black surface so scared
For the boys life Ben really cared
But he felt so unprepared

Chorus

Ben jumped in, hated the smell
Felt the cold water, thought of hell
Couldn"t swim, heard the death bell
And the crack of an egg shell

The little boy in a perfect swim
Saved Ben, holding his limb
Using all the little body's vim
Taking Ben out of the dim

Chorus

Little boy's mother came
Calling out his name
Ben told without shame
The little boy should have fame

Woman came on board that sunny day
Asked what Ben had to say
Ben asked if they wanted to stay
She said 'yes' without delay

Chorus

38. The tree

A week after I was born
In the very early morn
My mom took me to a tree
She laid me down and left me

Chorus
The branches over my head
Was naked for wintercold
I was alive, not dead
I was only one week old

On my 20th birthday
I brought a girl so sweet
On the grass she lay
I could hear my heart beat

Chorus
The branches over my head
Was soft green for spring
I was alive, not dead
My youth was the only thing

40 I reached
We came to the tree
My children I teached
What that tree meant to me

Chorus
The branches over my head
Was green summer hot
I was alive, not dead
Inside me was a blind spot

So 60 came
I was alone under that tree
I felt it was a shame
That nobody was there with me

Chorus
The branches over my head'
Was all orange and yellow
I was alive, not dead
I felt sad and mellow

80 - the last parade
Everyone was there
Friends, family, the whole arcade
We blew bubbles in the air

Chorus
The branches over my head
Was once again winter naked
I was alive, not dead
And my cocktail was stirred, not shaked

39. In front of a cafe

/:At man walks down the street:/
You can hear his high heels
Whenever he moves his feet

/:A woman, she is not from this part of town:/
You can see on her clothes
That she is not from here around

/:They will meet in front of the cafe where I sit:/
They will fall in love
And eventually they will split

40. **A rainy day somewhere**

Sam stood in the rain like he was crying
Joanna sat in the train reading her magazine
Louisa stepped out in the pouring rain tipping her toes
A buss somewhere gave a honk
Maria left her table in the small coffee shop not too happy

A car drove by and Sam jumped
He didn't have to, but it felt good
To jump in the pouring rain
Louisa and Maria saw the jumping man
Smiled at each other

Joanna sat in a train miles from these incidents
Never had a chance to see
Sam, Maria or Louisa in the pouring rain

In the city where Joanna sat on her train
Now waiting for a signal
The sun was shining

41. **Teacher said**

Goethes Werther suffered
And so did I
Like the hero in the book
I just wanted to die
I decided to deliever
My body to the river
Went down to river bed
Then I heard what my teacher said
She said; "Sit still, Antony
Don't drag Maria´s hair
Never bully the smaller classes
Always sit still on your chair
Pencils between index and thumb
Fox is red, hanes to bed, that is what the farmer said
You can call me Miss Hansen
Because that is my name
We will all learn how to write our names
Don't go down to the river bed
Count the eggs in the nest
It is going to be so much fun in school
School, cool, rule
Anton, please sit still and listen to your teacher"

Goethes Werther suffered
And so did I
Like the hero in the book

I wanted to die
The water was cold
As I drifted towards the waterfall
I saw clouds passed
Then again I heard
What the teacher said
"There are seven continents
Africa is hot
A squared + b squared = c squared where c is the hypotenuse
H.C. Andersen wrote about himself
Yellow are the colours of the taxis in New York City
There are many ways to write a poem
You shouldn't drown yourself because of a stupid book
How many times shall I tell you to sit still on your chair, Antony
The south american island Galapagos played a major role for Darwins evolution theory The birth of our civilisation lies in Greece
The nordic gods ate apples to keep them young"

"Don´t you dare drown yourself because of a stupid book"

I frowned
My spirit drowned
My teacher was real
She would bring me back to life
I was hit by a hook
My teacher on the shore
She was furious and bold
I was wet and cold
She didn't care about my way
She had so much to say
And it is quite absurd
To this day, I can't remember a word
Of that lesson I heard
Sitting by the the banks of the river
It was so cold, my body started to shiver
After the lesson
She told me to go home and be ashamed
So I went home, could not explain the wet cloths
And the hole in the sweater where the hook
Dragged me back to life

42. **It is clear**

You left me without a word
Just a drawing on the wall
So I screamed to be heard
Spitting images of fall

Chorus
My couch is cosy, my bed is warm
I try my best to do no harm
I pick up trash, I pick up gold
Getting wiser, getting old

So now as the end is near
I search for your body heat
White blankets full of fear
Fish and chips is all I eat

Chorus

This night as I opened my eyes
To see Invaders from the outer space
Their yellow skin threatening me
My body is numb, so is my face

Chorus

Bleeding softness into the air
I sense no strings of hope
Bodies lying everywhere
I saw it in a telescope

43. **BZ**

Teargas in the hallway
Blinded naked youth
They gave us few uptions
To see the morning truth

So we held our hands neatly
Gave them a freedom song
They beated hell out of us
Couldn't cut our tongue

We gave them nothing
Relied only on what we knew
The screams left unheard
On the edge, loving the view

44. Open your eyes, stranger!

As the refugee opens his eyes
he stares into wild waves
of horrified intruders
fear is hammered into his brain
loneliness is the currency here
he is longing for home
his fist firmly tight
closes the gap
between reality and dream
when somebody shows him
an open door and a friendly face
it is too late as the fist
meets the mild breeze of salty sea

In the news it was a headline
from 4 pm to 5.30 pm

'A young man from the southern hemisphere drowned
himself in the ocean'

45. In between reality

Sliced through my thoughts of inferior
My mind and spirit were low
Didn´t have anything to care for
Didn´t have anywhere to go
Saw my reflections fading
And the child leaving for good
Animals in the alley invading
Like it was understood

Chorus
That I owe it to yesterday
Tomorrow will bring another day

Heroes dying just for fun
No reason to be seen or heard
Going to work every morn´
Evening applepie for dessert
Lying in bed all alone
Listening to the other heartbeat
Sinking like a white stone
In the tropical night heat

Chorus
Oh I owe it to yesterday
Tomorrow will bring another day

In the reality I attended
People had that naked look
Where love and fear never ended
Untill the original captain Hook
Was staring with one eye
At the nun and her vagina
Who never had told a lie
Coming all the way from China

Chorus

When the sun finally collapsed
The Instagram broke down
As the time slowly elapsed
Everybody wanted the crown
"I took the best and final shot
Of the star burning bright"
in a flash it was extremely hot
And then came eternal night

Chorus

46. In France there was no regret

Morning came with sun and heat
In southern France I felt the beat
Marseille, Toulouse and fair Orange
I knew it was a golden chance
So I traveled the Provence style
And held my breath with a smile
Danced on a lavender field
Rain made the purple so unreal

Chorus
In dreamy France there was no regret
une belle femme enchantè
Sur le promenad et dans la fêté

Noon arrived with much delight
Five courses made us feel alright
Food and wine and lots of fun
We were all youngsters on the run
Conversations dull and full of taste
It was the most wonderful waste
of time and life and love
With the provencial sun high above

Chorus

Endless dreams of a future bright
Singing "Hurricane" in the fading light
Love was in the air and in the wine
Even 'le patron' was gentle and kind
"Tomorrow is another working day"
We agreed in our own French way
Kissed and hugged in the cold
Never thought we could get old

Chorus

47. Edinburgh a Hgrubnide

When the joy went for a ride
I went into a tea shop to wait
I called your name as soft as I could
You entered shaking your head

You told me to go outside and listen
To the sounds of the town
So I stepped outside just to hear
Sounds from a merry go round

Cars and busses off course
Two friends in a serious chat
The scream of a hungry seagull
A bagpipe on top of that

Chorus
In the town I talk about
The people don´t scream and shout
That it could be one of the best
Places to be – they just smile and rest

I look around to discover
If there is anything in it for me
On a cliff a castle so majestic
I was too scared to see

My friend said hey, let´s go
Hold my hand so gentle and warm
The April sun made it all clear
This town has its own charm

In the park in front of the station
You find a steeple just for fun
John Byrne draw a smoking cigarette
And a man on the wildest run

Chorus
Drinking honey golden whisky
Smiles made my day sunny
I laughed all night long
You kept calling me Johnny

When I woke up
With a hangover cold
My voice was harsh
And I felt so old

My tea shop offered
A tea and a smile
We watched the parade
On the Royal Mile

Chorus

48. New York, New York, funky version

Chorus
New York, New York
Everybody is looking for New York, New York
Can't seem to find it
Chorus: Sad story. Why not?
Me: Too crowded
Chorus: What is going on?
Me: All these people, they are all looking for
New York, New York
Everybody is looking for New York, New York

Times Square
I was there
I read a book
People had that look
That man is insane to be found there
Nobody reads books on Times Square
But I can tell you, I did
Can´t remember a shit
Of what happened in the book
I only remember the look
Of people passing by
Give it a try

Chorus

I saw a guy
Never asked why
On his back
Sat a pack

Of rats so real
You could feel
Stinking toes
One never knows
Where those rats in the light
Had spend their night
I asked him about those rats
Said something about stinking fats
And laughed
(shouldn´t have done that, wasn't polite)
He punched my nose, and danced like Clay
And right there on that street, that day
I found something that made me glad
I think Cassius thought that I´d gone mad
Doctors came to pick me up
Saw my broken nose, had a shock
But I was smiling like the happiest man
None of the doctors did understand
When I was lying flat on the street
With a broken nose and a swollen feet
I found something I was searching for
From the bottom and up: New York

Chorus
Breathe in and out
Breathe in and out
Breathe in and out
This is live and shout
But in New York
People only breathe out

Chorus

49. I aint gonna work for the US government no more

No, I aint gonna work for the US government no more
No, I aint gonna work for the US government no more
I am a federal worker
And my name pay no rent
I am a usual suspect
Doing work for government
Its a shame the way they make me scrub the floor
I aint gonna work for the US government no more

No, I aint gonna work for the US government no more
No, I aint gonna work for the US government no more
They hand you a nickel
they hand you a dime
They ask you with a grin
If you are having a good time
They have borrowed every cent, can't borrow anymore
I aint gonna work for the US government no more

No, I aint gonna work for the US government no more
No, I aint gonna work for the US government no more
It is chinese business men
That decide if i get paid
I feel like I am a hooker
Just waiting to get laid
The National Guard stands around my door
I aint gonna work for the US government no more

No, I aint gonna work for the US government no more

No, I aint gonna work for the US government no more
I dreamed of all the good things
That I could do for my land
Why I should work for the chinese
I just don't understand
They say get yourself another IPhone and I just get bored
I aint gonna work for the US government no more

No, I aint gonna work for the US government no more
No, I aint gonna work for the US government no more
I gonna quit my job
Going to live out on the street
So many of us out there
Happy on our feet
The underworld has all the answers we are looking for
I aint gonna work for the US government no more

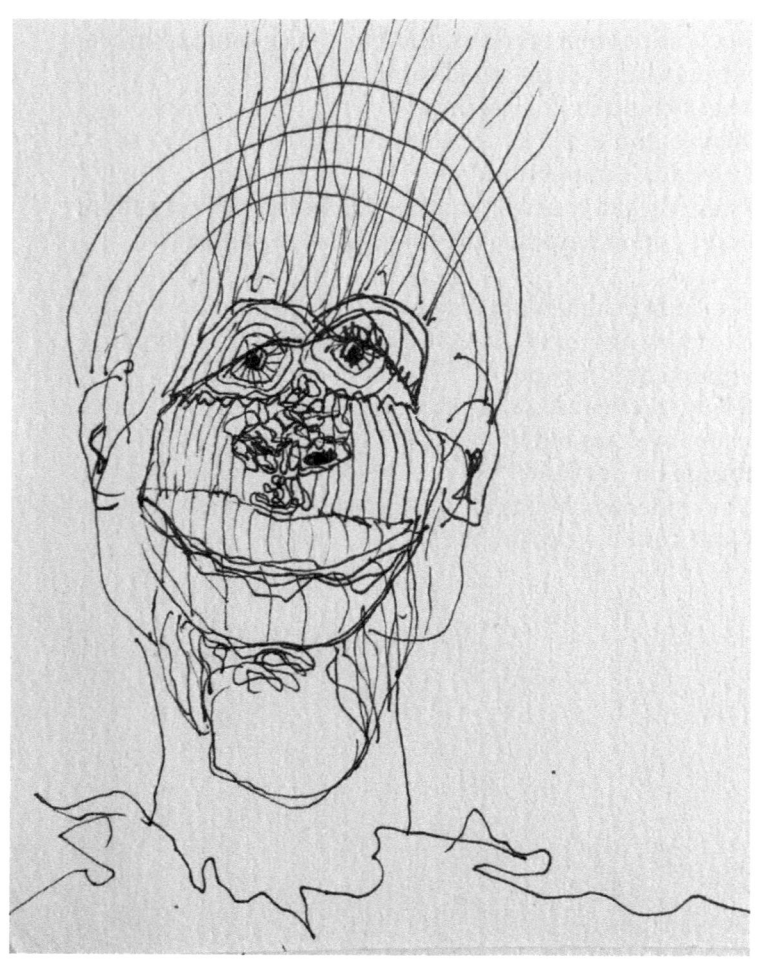

Iluustration by Alice Fernbank

50. **Red haired giant**

Red haired lady
Giant so neat and cute
Called out love with a song
And a dancing tribute

She flew across the sea
And landed on her feet
She came all the way to me
Dancing in the street

A soft kiss she blew
Like a whirling butterfly
I thumpled to the ground and knew
Nothing but the dear blue sky

I walked the walls of fear
Called an army to defend
Now whenever she is near
My heart is so easily bend

The night is young
And the fear is old
She is pure and strong
And her hair shines like gold

So mates, call out for fun
Sing an ode for real joy
She became my loving one
To take care of me and my boy

51. Blind trust

In heaven of blind trust
And sad memories
I saw you coming
It blew my mind
In a split second
To last forever

The strength of
Your fortune
And your will
To let it be
Gave me something
To hold me on to

Chorus
Then you said something
I never heard
Because your smile
Made me tingle inside

I fell from the sky
Into the black gold
Water of distrust
From yesterdays
Defined
Misbehaving

I reached out for you
Only to find
A glooming star
So near
And yet
So far away

Chorus

It will take me years
I know that now
To open
My heart
Completely
For you

And while I find the strength
To do that I hope your
Light will shine into
The black ocean
As the beautiful
Star I love

Chorus

52. **Buzzard**

A buzzard floating on hot air
So many times I dreamed being there
So majestic doing so little
Just hanging there playing its fiddle

Often I imagined how it would be
What it was the royal bird did see
I dreamed of an intense and glorified view
Fields of gold and a sky so blue

One day I heard the cry of the bird
A really sad sound I heard
No royal roar or thunder
It was a sad cry from deep down under

It was as the buzzard would say
That this was just another sad day
Nothing to brag about or make a big noise
And therefore the buzzard used the tiniest voice

53. Pure gold

Midnight angels flaming
Pure as solid gold
We saw the future fading
!:Into a widescreen color show:!

While depressed mothers were talking
About nothing and their clothes
We were to understand and
!:Accept the final blow.!

When the silent crowd collapsed
And walls fell to the ground
The human sacrifice
:!Made a sad coceiling sound:!

We were two bodies rolling
Cuddling un a graveyeard
There was nothing we could do
!:To make a better start:!